PUZZLE JOURNEY UNDER THE SEA

Lesley Sims
Illustrated by Sue Stitt

Designed by Lucy Parris
Edited by Jenny Tyler
Marine biology consultant: Dr. Brian Bett
Diving consultant: Reg Vallintine

Aquamarina
FREE PASS
Name: Ally
Samuels
(with Dr. & Prof. Samuels)

Aquamarina
FREE PASS
Name: Dirk
Samuels
(with Dr. & Prof. Samuels)

marina
PASS
Name: Jon
Samuels
(with Dr. & Prof. Samuels)

Dear Reader,

This book tells the story of an incredible underwater adventure I had with my brothers Jon and Dirk. It all began at Aquamarina, a sort of ocean museum. Our parents were at a conference there. We thought it would be boring but we had an amazing time. Turn the page to join us.

Ally Samuels

Aquamarina

"Have fun! Be good!" Dad called, already deep in his conference papers. "Fun? In a museum?" Jon asked.

"It's better than sitting in boring lectures," said Dirk. "But we can't look at pictures of fish *all* day."

"Hey!" cried Jon, spotting a sign for sunken treasure. He raced ahead. That sounded more exciting.

The *Dolphin*'s Captain, Ferdinand Smith.

These jars hold perfumed oil. The *Dolphin* was carrying 15 of these when it went down.

THE *DOLPHIN*

Built in 1598, it was struck by lightning on its very first voyage and sank to the bottom of the sea. *Where does it lie? Nobody knows.*

It carried 9 treasure chests in the hold, all full of fabulous jewels.

STATUE OF NEPTUNE

On board the *Dolphin* was this incredible statue. It was carved from a very rare green marble.

We think the statue looked like this.

Neptune's hand was the only thing found. It is being studied here in the museum by Prof. Theo Turtle.

But when we joined him, all we saw was a display board. We read it anyway. It told an amazing story.

A ship called the *Dolphin* had sunk. All of its precious cargo was lost, except for one hand from a statue.

The hand looked creepy on its own. "Do you think the ship and treasure are still down there?" said Dirk.

2

"You bet!" cried a voice, making us jump. "Are you Ally, Jon and Dirk?" asked a friendly face. I nodded.

"Hi, I'm Theo," she said. "I work here. Your parents told me to keep an eye out for you. I need your help."

We followed Theo as she explained. "I'm going on a search for the *Dolphin* and I'm looking for a crew."

We were ready to set sail on the spot. "It's OK with your parents," Theo said, "but my crew must be sharp-eyed and quick-witted. I can't take just anyone with me."

She unrolled a map. "Here's a puzzle to test your seafaring skills. If you can tell me which ports are listed, you're hired."

Can you help us?

Ports
Each port is shown by a letter and a number. To find the port at D11, go up line 'D' until it meets the line going across it numbered 11.

Port Fjord

Port Russe

Green Port

South Port

Gold Port

King Port

Port Prince

Port of Plenty

Rock Port

Bay Port

Port Point

Port Cape

Port Hope

B8
D3
G7
K6

This map belongs to F. Smith 1597

All aboard!

We raced through the names, eager to start. Theo's ship was floating in an indoor pool by her lab. "It's the fastest ship at sea!" she said. "There's no ship like it."

Dirk wanted to try all the controls. "What's that?" Jon asked, looking at a tall glass jar. "My Undersea Scanner," said Theo. "It's going to help us find the *Dolphin*."

"I have a hand from a statue on board the ship. If we can find the statue, I think we'll find the wreck."

"Look!" She put the hand into the jar. "The scanner can identify what stone the hand is made from."

"Then, if I click the *Search* button, the computer will tell the ship where to find more of the same stone."

This ship's faster than a rocket!

"Here goes!" she said and clicked *Search*. We dived underwater, shot from the dock and into the sea.

Suddenly, a huge face filled the porthole. We were on a headfirst collision course with a sea lion.

With seconds to spare, it swerved away. "Welcome to the Galapagos Islands," said Theo.

4

"All these fish," said Dirk. "And they're coming right up to the ship!"

"They're curious," Theo explained. "They don't see many people."

Penguins dived after fish as dolphins rolled over in front of us. I made friends with a sea lion through the glass. "Hey, a swimming lizard!" cried Jon. "It's a marine iguana," Theo said.

Underneath us and the ship, some sharks were lying on a reef. All of a sudden, I realized I could see part of the statue.

Can you spot it?

Seaweed safari

But with it on board, we saw that it was only the base and a foot. The rest of the statue was nowhere in sight. There was no sign of the *Dolphin* either.

"We've hardly started!" Theo cried, clicking *Search* again. A message flashed up: *Next stop, San Diego.*

All at once, we were in an undersea forest. Seaweed as big as trees stretched high above us. Theo was telling us about it when an otter zoomed past. "Can we follow him?" Dirk asked.

"OK," said Theo. She weaved the ship in and out of the tangled weed. On the surface, the otters were wrapped up in weeds. They floated lazily on their backs, eating.

The otters were using their fronts as tables. They smashed open shells with rocks and guzzled the contents. "Neat trick!" said Jon. "But I'd prefer a burger."

"We must get on," Theo said. "The computer says the rest of the statue is here somewhere." She pulled a lever and the ship dived back down.

The seaweed is called kelp. It's used to make all sorts of things, even ice cream!

As we searched for the statue, we saw all kinds of fish. Theo told us their names as they swam past.

"Will you help me to count the fish and sharks for my research?" she asked.

We agreed, but it wasn't easy because the fish didn't stay still.

Dirk counted sharks. He could only see one. Theo pointed to a shape like a glider on the sea bed.

"That's an angel shark. It half-buries itself in the sand to ambush its prey."

How many angel sharks can you find? Can you spot 9 fringeheads, 4 batrays, 7 kelpfish and 2 eels?

Flying fish and a find

Dirk didn't only find sharks. He spotted a piece of the statue, caught in the kelp.

With it safe on board, Theo clicked *Search* and we sped to the Caribbean.

Sunshine flooded the ship. All around us, flying fish soared over the sea.

The computer beeped. It had sensed something. Was it the *Dolphin*?

We scrambled into the wetsuits and other diving gear Theo found for us.

Dirk had a struggle getting his fins on. "The tank of air's too heavy," he puffed.

As we dived through the water, a shape shimmered below us. It was a sunken galleon!

Full of excitement, we swam closer. Dirk was all set, with a special noteboard. He could write things underwater, and his notes wouldn't be soggy.

Jon snapped away using a waterproof camera. It was specially made, to be easy to use in the ocean.

Theo took a sand blower to blast sand safely from the wreck. Lurking behind the clouds of sand, she spotted something.

It was a dirty lump of metal. But beneath the dirt, gold gleamed: treasure – and still shaped like a chest, even though its box had rotted.

We found cutlasses and cannons too. It wasn't the *Dolphin* but we guessed who used to sail this ship. **Can you?**

I can see a piece of the statue!

A town underwater

Back on the ship, we looked at the 'statue'. It was in a sorry state. "It must have broken and spread throughout the oceans," Theo said.

Just then, the computer flashed a message. *Stone in a building in Port Royal.* The printer chattered into life. A map of a town came out.

"This is Port Royal," said Theo. "Hundreds of years ago, there was a terrible earthquake here. The town of Port Royal sank into the sea."

In a tavern, there were tankards all over the floor.

The place where we'd find the stone was marked on the map. We studied it, looking out over the town. Then we pulled on diving gear and set off to explore.

It felt strange, swimming where people used to walk. We followed fish in and out of the buildings. We even found things which had survived the earthquake.

But only one of us knew where the piece of statue was. The other two hadn't held the map the right way up, on Theo's ship.

Who knew where to go?

Rig robots

Leaving the watery town behind, the ship took us on to the cold, grey North Sea.

We stopped near a giant oil rig, sinking down beside a massive leg. The sea was very murky.

We could just make out some divers hard at work. "That's unusual," said Theo. "These days, most underwater jobs are carried out by robots."

"The robots are called Remotely Operated Vehicles – R.O.V.s for short. They can do all kinds of jobs. Some collect things. Some have cameras."

She watched a diver on a grid. "Now, he's saying something very interesting."

I couldn't hear anything. "How do you know?" I asked.

"Well, divers normally talk to each other over microphones, but he's using hand signs," Theo replied.

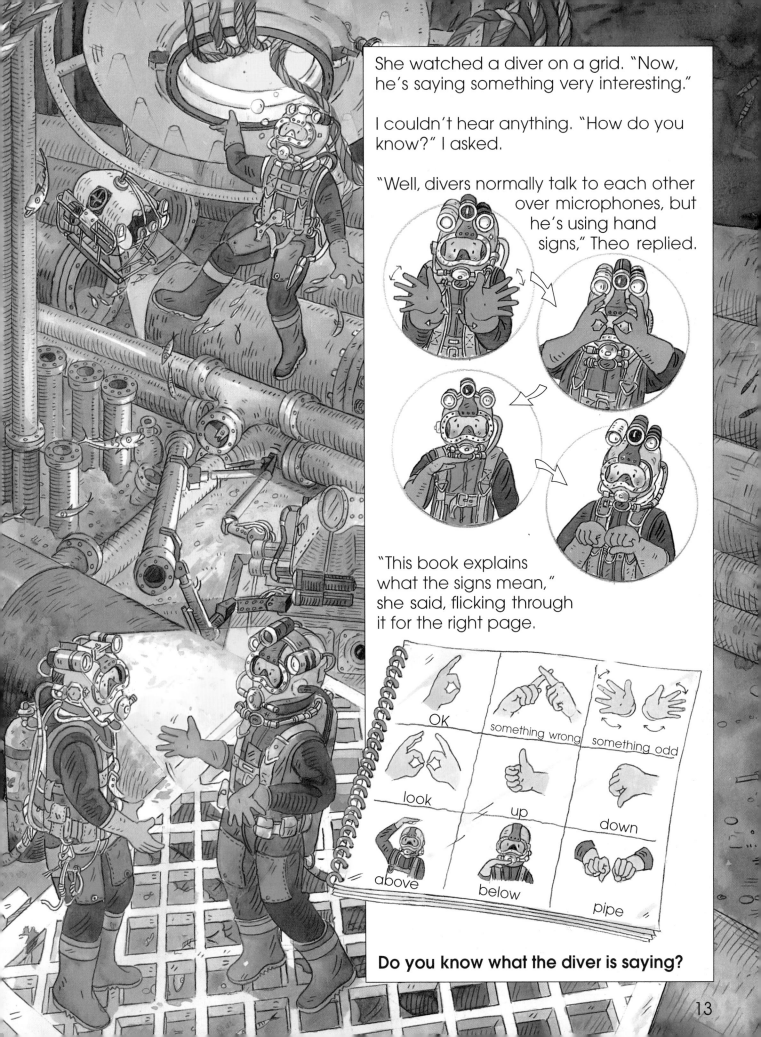

"This book explains what the signs mean," she said, flicking through it for the right page.

OK	something wrong	something odd
look	up	down
above	below	pipe

Do you know what the diver is saying?

Deep down

The sharp-eyed diver had spotted a marble right hand and arm. We took it on board. The next thing we knew, the sea outside was pitch black. We had moved on again. The ship sank deeper into the ocean.

Theo switched on the ship's headlights. The weirdest fish swam past us. One had a light on its head!

"The sun can't reach this far down, so they have to make their own light," Theo explained. "It makes it very cold too."

There is stone in a valley in the Mid-Atlantic ridge.

The ship landed gently on the sea floor. "These are the abyssal plains," said Theo. "Years ago, we thought nothing could live here. These fish have had to adapt to the cold and the dark and little food."

As she spoke, a message came up on screen. "The Mid-Atlantic ridge!" Jon said. "We did this at school. It's part of the longest mountain range in the world and it's all underwater."

Swiftly, Theo turned the ship. We rose up a rocky slope and then dipped down sharply. Coming down the side of the mountain, we entered a deep valley.

To our surprise, the first thing we saw were chimneys. "They're black smokers," Theo told us. "The 'smoke' is really hot water shooting out of the earth. Minerals in the water make it black."

"I can see a piece of statue!" Jon interrupted. Then Theo saw it too. But she looked puzzled.

Can you see it? What is odd about it?

An icy maze

Another left hand? Feeling confused, we collected it. Seconds later, we were afloat in a white, icy landscape.

"This must be the Antarctic," I cried, spotting some penguins.

But with the help of Theo's binoculars, Dirk saw something better. "There's a piece of the statue! It's frozen in some ice."

"Everyone on lookout duty," called Theo. "Help me find a way through the ice to it, and then out to open sea."

Can you find the way?

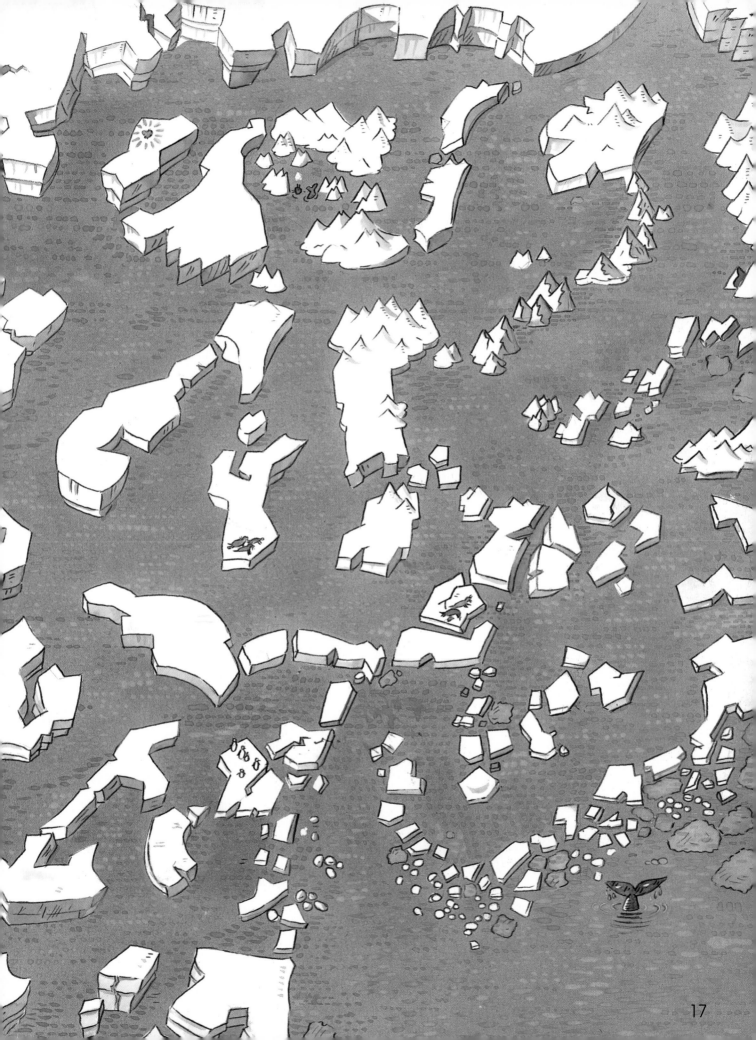

The amazing changing cuttlefish

It's like being a miner!

Adding a marble leg to our collection, we sailed on, to the coast of Tasmania.

"We'll explore an underwater cave here," said Theo, finding equipment. Jon tried on a hard hat for size. Dirk was given a reel and line to wind.

"Look out for cuttlefish too," Theo added. "They can change themselves to hide from enemies like dolphins."

Excitedly, we eased our way through the exit hatch into the sea.

Theo tied one end of her line to a rock outside a cave. Then she checked it.

We'd need to follow the line coming back, or we might never find a way out.

Deep in the cave, clusters of eggs hung from the roof. As we swam in, a baby cuttlefish was hatching. *About turn!* Theo mimed and led us out. She wanted us to leave the babies in peace.

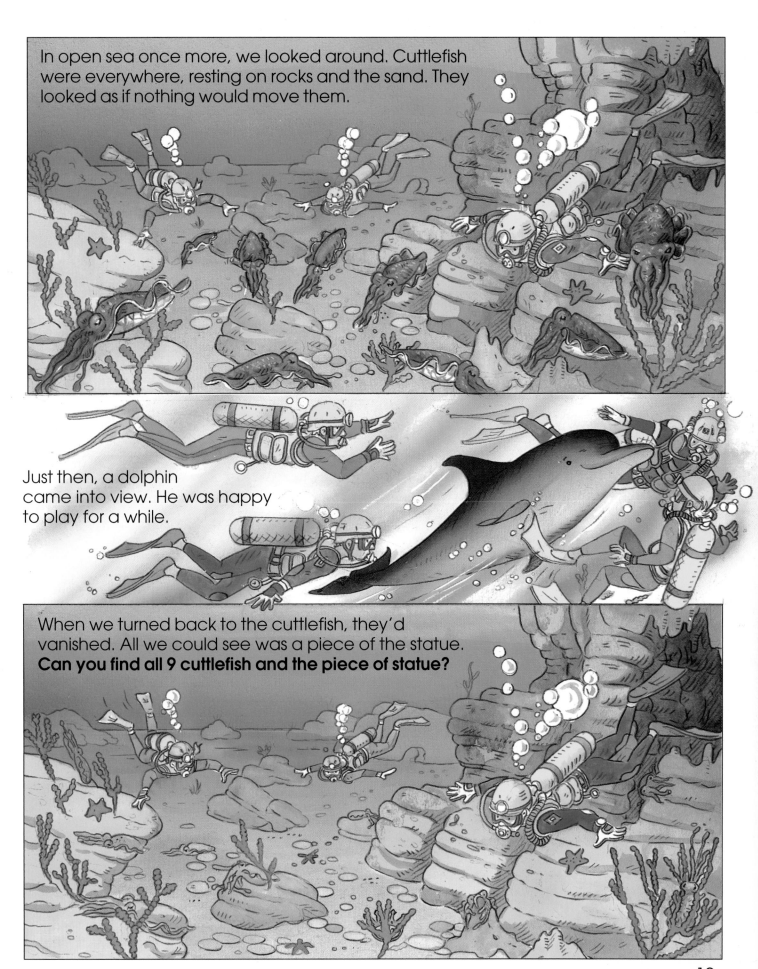

In open sea once more, we looked around. Cuttlefish were everywhere, resting on rocks and the sand. They looked as if nothing would move them.

Just then, a dolphin came into view. He was happy to play for a while.

When we turned back to the cuttlefish, they'd vanished. All we could see was a piece of the statue.
Can you find all 9 cuttlefish and the piece of statue?

Anemone search

Hooking up the crown, we set off for the Great Barrier Reef. At once, the computer sent another message: *The stone is by a pink-striped anemone.*

"You three dive in to look for it and I'll follow on with the ship," Theo said. "Anemones have long tentacles, like fingers. Stripy fish are often nearby."

A ray was at Jon's heels as he floated over a crown of thorns starfish. It looked like a cross between a spiky cactus plant and a spider.

But Jon was watching a fish have its teeth cleaned. Two sea snakes spotted Dirk. He stayed still as stone as they looked him over.

I swam beside a turtle. The water wasn't very deep. You could see the bottom of Theo's boat above us and the sea bed below.

Then we swam over to a strange-looking fish.

All at once, it blew up like a prickly balloon and took off.

Startled, we let it flee, gazing instead into a giant clam.

We had so much fun we forgot everything . . . until Dirk held up his waterproof board.

Trying to remember Theo's description, we hunted around for the stone and the striped anemone.

Can you see them?

A cargo of tea

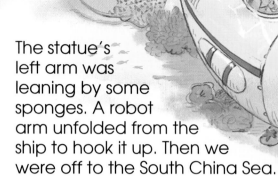

The statue's left arm was leaning by some sponges. A robot arm unfolded from the ship to hook it up. Then we were off to the South China Sea.

Pointed lines on one of the scanners showed it had detected metal. "Another wreck?" Dirk's eyes shone.

But there was no sign of a wreck, just fish, swarming around a hole in the sea bed.

Theo put on the ship's lights. There was a big, rusty anchor sticking out of the mud.

We dived in to investigate. Theo showed Dirk how to use a water jet. A long, snaky hose attached it to a pump on board.

Firing the jet, Dirk began to clear the mud. But there was still no wreck. All we saw were a few scattered crates.

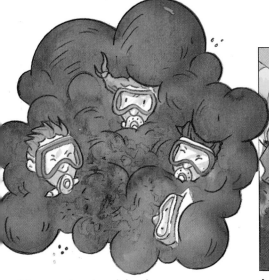

Theo started to lever one out of the mud. At once, we were engulfed in a dense, black cloud.

As it cleared, we realized the crates had rotted. Whatever was inside, now sat in thick, muddy sludge.

Theo scooped handfuls of the sludge and its contents into bags. We took muddy armfuls back to the ship.

"This is fantastic!" said Theo, back on board. We were baffled. It looked like a pile of old mud to us.

"It's the cargo of a merchant ship!" Theo exclaimed. "They took tea, silks and china to Europe. That black cloud around us was ancient tea leaves!"

"We must keep the china wet," she added, "because it's been underwater so long. If it dries out, it will become fragile. It might even crumble. We'll clean it up properly when we get back to Aquamarina. But let's try to list what we've found."

We could tell what things were from the parts which showed through the mud. One object looked very out of place.

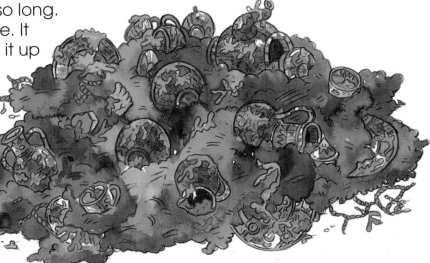

What objects can you see?

Locked in a box

So now we had the other foot. But we hadn't seen even a plank from the *Dolphin*. Onto our next port of call – the Indian Ocean.

Theo was telling us about nearby coral islands, when a strange message came up on the screen. "Is the scanner broken?" I said.

But everything looked OK. Jon hovered at Theo's elbow. "Theo, can I take a photo of a coral island?" he asked. Theo nodded.

The view from the dome was spectacular. Jon aimed, ready to snap. . .

. . .when a bird swooped down. It snatched the camera from his grasp.

The bird flew off over an island. It dropped the camera deep into the sea.

The rope keeps the divers in a straight line. It helps them to search an area thoroughly.

"Oh no!" Jon was horrified. Every picture – sunk. "All's not lost," said Theo. "We'll use a swim line to find it."

We were puzzled, until she explained. A swim line was a rope that helped divers to search for things.

"I'll take the ship to just above where the camera was dropped. Then we'll start our search," she said.

24

"Before we go, remember these signals. One tug on the rope means *go*, two mean *stop*. Three mean *stop, I've seen something.*"

She anchored the rope by a peg and we spread out, loosely holding onto the rope. At a sharp tug from Theo, we began.

We swept around in a broad circle. I spotted the camera nestling in some coral and quickly pulled the rope: *one, two, three*!

Out of water, it weighs a ton.

No sooner had I moved to get the camera, than the rope was yanked again. Dirk had found something too: an old, battered box.

We heaved it on board, only to find it locked. But it didn't need a key. Instead it had dials in the lid, like a combination lock.

The numbers made a pattern. But two dials were wrong. To open the box, we had to put them right. **Which dials are wrong?**

25

The final piece?

To our astonishment, the box sprang back to reveal a chunk of statue. "Talk about a lucky coincidence!" said Theo, hitting *Search*.

In the Red Sea, the computer pinpointed more stone, inside a wreck. This was the biggest so far, a huge, metal ship lying on its side. At first, we swam from stern to bow around the outside.

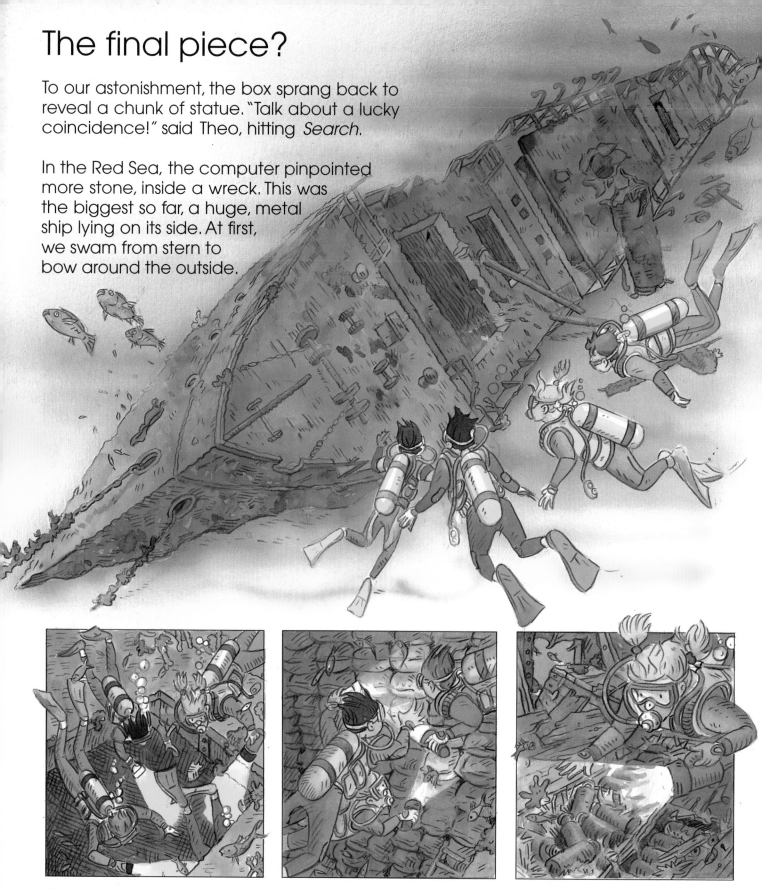

Flicking on flashlights, we followed Theo in. She led us through an open hatch, into the holds below.

In the first, we saw row upon row of sacks. They had stuck together fast, as hard and solid as a wall.

In another, I found wooden crates. Old glass bottles winked up at me, still packed in straw.

But in the last hold was the best, most surprising discovery of all – two old-fashioned cars.

I caught a glimpse of a face by a wheel. It wasn't a mermaid . . . was it? Curious, I swam over. I'd found the statue's head!

But Theo wasn't excited. "A day's searching and we're no nearer to the *Dolphin*," she said glumly.

Dirk tried to cheer her up. "We must have all of the statue by now," he said. "Can we stick it together to see?" He had no idea of the surprise in store.

Can you see how it fits together?

Statue surprise

Imagine our amazement. A stunning statue lay before us – but it wasn't Neptune. All we had of him was the left hand which had started our search.

That's why we had two left hands!

More stone in the wreck the computer insisted. Puzzled, Theo looked again with an X-ray camera.

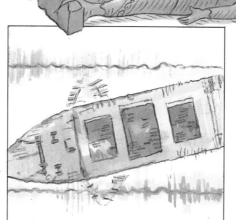

Faint behind the main wreck was a ghostly outline. Could there be a second ship underneath?

Theo moved the sand by the first wreck with an airlift. It worked like an undersea vacuum cleaner.

Strut by strut, a wooden frame appeared, followed by a half-buried chest. Hardly daring to hope, we read the name on the lid. *The Dolphin*. At last!

Then the work really began. Theo laid a special grid over the wreck. We had to measure, sketch and take a photo of every single thing before we could move it.

Huge lifting bags like hot air balloons carried everything up to the surface.

Theo brought the ship up and we formed a chain to load our finds on board.

We'd found all nine treasure chests, nine oil jars and something in a sack.

"Neptune?" cried Jon. It *had* to be. Sure enough, the left hand was missing. But the base was broken too.

In a flash, Dirk leapt up. "Try it with the other statue!" he said. We dragged it over. They fitted together like a jigsaw. Theo was thrilled.

"We've found nearly everything!" she said. "Just six oil jars missing." She paused. "And I think we might have passed those on our way."

Look back at the seas we visited. Can you spot the missing jars?

Our route

This is the route we took. We looked up
the things we saw in Theo's books.

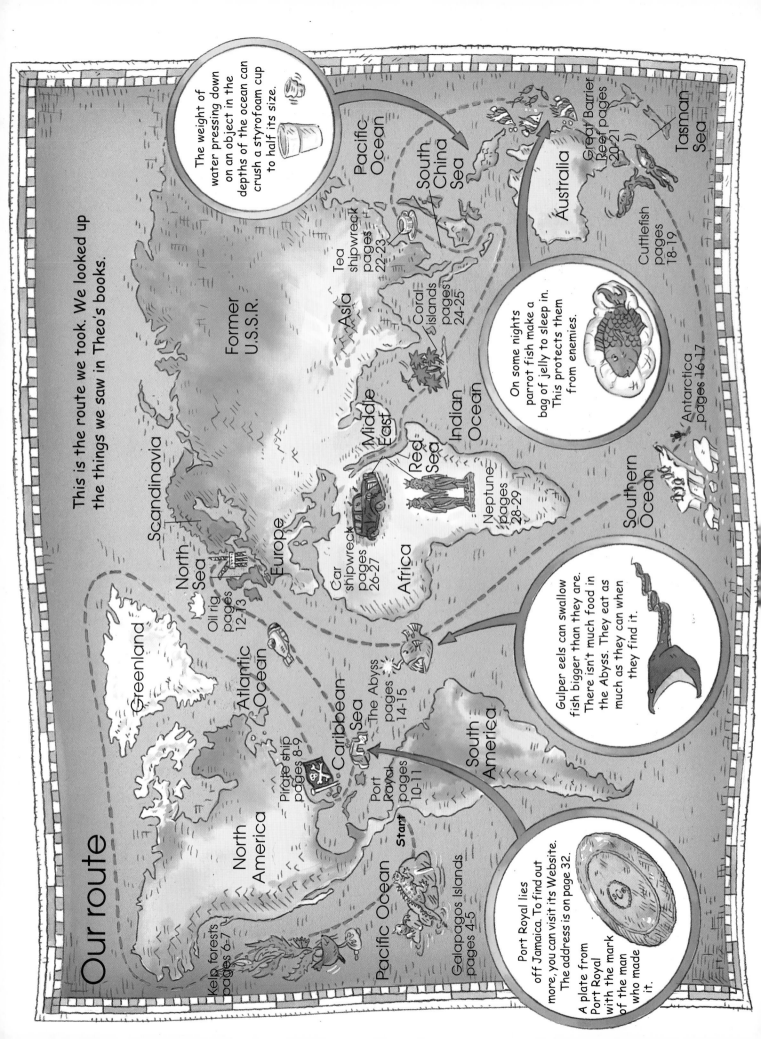

The weight of water pressing down on an object in the depths of the ocean can crush a styrofoam cup to half its size.

Pacific Ocean

South China Sea

Tea shipwreck pages 22-23

Asia

Coral Islands pages 24-25

Former U.S.S.R.

Australia

Great Barrier Reef pages 20-21

Tasman Sea

Cuttlefish pages 18-19

On some nights parrot fish make a bag of jelly to sleep in. This protects them from enemies.

Antarctica pages 16-17

Scandinavia

Europe

Middle East

Red Sea

Indian Ocean

Neptune pages 28-29

Africa

Car shipwreck pages 26-27

Southern Ocean

North Sea

Oil rig pages 12-13

Greenland

Atlantic Ocean

Caribbean Sea

The Abyss pages 14-15

Pirate ship pages 8-9

Port Royal pages 10-11

South America

Gulper eels can swallow fish bigger than they are. There isn't much food in the Abyss. They eat as much as they can when they find it.

North America

Kelp forests pages 6-7

Pacific Ocean

Start

Galapagos Islands pages 4-5

Port Royal lies off Jamaica. To find out more, you can visit its Website. The address is on page 32.

A plate from Port Royal with the mark of the man who made it.

Answers

pages 2-3
Aquamarina

The ports are:
B8 – Gold Port   D3 – Port Cape
G7 – Port of Plenty   K6 – Bay Port

pages 4-5
All aboard!

The piece of statue is here.

pages 6-7 Seaweed safari

The angel sharks are numbered 1-4. The fringeheads are ringed in green. The batrays are ringed in black. The kelpfish are ringed in blue. The eels are ringed in red.

pages 8-9
Flying fish and a find

The ship was sailed by pirates. You can see a skull and crossbones on this barrel.

pages 10-11
A town underwater

Ally knew where to find the stone. She held her map the right way, so it matched the layout of the town.

pages 12-13
Rig robots

The diver is saying, "Something odd. Look below pipe." He has seen a marble hand.

pages 14-15
Deep down

Here's the piece of statue. But it's a left hand and they have one already. Theo put it in her Undersea Scanner.

pages 16-17
An icy maze

Their route is shown in black. The piece of statue is here.

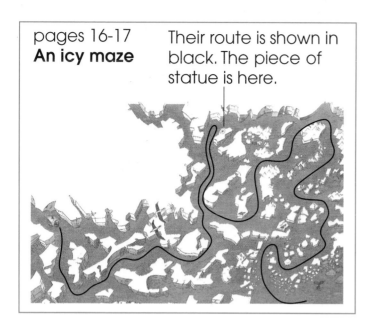

pages 18-19
The amazing changing cuttlefish

The cuttlefish have been numbered 1 to 9. The piece of statue they found was the crown. It is ringed in black.

pages 20-21
Anemone search

The pink-striped anemone and the piece of statue are ringed.

pages 22-23
A cargo of tea

cups
bowls
plate
foot
vase
teapot lid
cup
plate
cup
jugs
plates

pages 24-25
Locked in a box

These dials are wrong: *a* *b*

The bottom number of one dial is the first number at the top of the next dial. Reading down, dial *a* = 4 5 6 and dial *b* = 8 9 0.

pages 26-27
The final piece?

When the statue is pieced together, it looks like this.

pages 28-29
Statue surprise

There are oil jars on pages:
6-7, 8-9, 10-11, 12-13, 20-21, and 24-25.

About Port Royal: Not all of Port Royal has been excavated. Our picture shows how it might look when it is. The Port Royal website is at: nautarch.tamu.edu/ projects/prhome.htm

Thanks to: Dr. D.L. Hamilton of Texas A & M University and Joe Pedley.

U.E. Printed in Portugal. First published in America 1999.